This Is Me and This Is Pip

Written and illustrated by Sally Symes

Collins

This is me, and this is Pip.
I like to jump. He likes to skip.

Pip skips up. I jump down.
Then we spin round and round.

We run, we hop. He skips, I jump.
It's lots of fun. Thud, thump and bump!

We see a swing up in the tree,
Pip sits on it, and shouts out ...

Cheep! Buzz! We look up in the tree.
Pip sees a nest. I see a bee.

We look and see a lot of bugs.
Ants and snails and ugly slugs!

We see the sand. We like to dig.
Pip is teeny. I am big!

The sun is hot, we see the pool.
Splishy, splashy! It feels cool.

We play at tag, and I am "it".
We run around, we must be fit!

The wind is flapping at the sheet,
I see Pip. I see his feet!

A puff of wind, a rainy cloud.
A flash, a crash! It's very loud.

It is raining. It's no fun.
Pip skips off, but I will run!

14

Ideas for reading

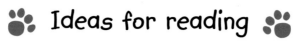

Written by Clare Dowdall, PhD
Lecturer and Primary Literacy Consultant

Learning objectives: read simple words by sounding out and blending the phonemes all through the word from left to right; read some high frequency words; read a range of familiar and common words and simple sentences independently; use phonic knowledge to write simple regular words; extend their vocabulary, exploring the meanings and sounds of new words; use talk to organise, sequence and clarify thinking, ideas, feelings and events

Curriculum links: Understanding the World: The world

Focus phonemes: y, zz, sh, th (this, thump), ai, ee, oo (boot, look), ou (round)

Fast words: me, like, I, we

Word count: 171

Getting started

- Revisit the focus phonemes using flash cards.

- Write the words *jump* and *skip* on a whiteboard. Identify the phoneme for each grapheme. Rehearse blending the phonemes in each word to read the word fluently.

- Look at the front cover and read the title aloud together. Discuss what is happening in the picture and what might happen in the book.

- Turn to the blurb. Model how to read the lines with expression, emphasising the rhythm and the rhyming words. Discuss which words rhyme. Ask children to suggest other words that would rhyme with *Pip* and *skip*, e.g. chip, nip.

Reading and responding

- Read pp2–3 as a group. Discuss what the children are doing and suggest what games they might be playing.

- Look at the word *round*. Introduce the digraph *ou* and help children to add sound buttons to this word on a whiteboard.

- Read pp4–5 together. Help children to sound out and blend the phonemes in longer words with digraphs and adjacent consonants, e.g. *th-u-m-p*. Model rereading whole sentences and rhyming sections with fluency.

- Ask children to continue to read to p13. Support them to tackle longer words and to reread sentences fluently.